SADDAM HUSSEIN

By Jill C. Wheeler

VISIT US AT
WWW.ABDOPUB.COM

Published by ABDO & Daughters, an imprint of ABDO Publishing Company, 4940 Viking Drive, Suite 622, Edina, Minnesota 55435.

Printed in the United States.

Edited by: Tamara L. Britton and Kate A. Conley
Graphic Design: Arturo Leyva, David Bullen
Cover Design: Castaneda Dunham, Inc.
Photos: AP/Wide World, Corbis

Library of Congress Cataloging-in-Publication Data

Wheeler, Jill C., 1964-
　　Saddam Hussein / Jill C. Wheeler.
　　　　p. cm. -- (War in Iraq)
　　Includes index.
　　Summary: A biography of Iraqi President Saddam Hussein, from his childhood to "Operation Iraqi Freedom," a battle waged by the United States and its allies intended to drive Hussein from Iraq.
　　Contents: A fight to the end -- Childhood poverty -- A dream of Arab unity -- Exile -- Young revolutionary -- A new agenda -- War with Iran -- Invading Kuwait -- Rebuilding -- Contained -- Loyalty or death -- Axis of evil -- Under attack.
　　ISBN 1-59197-499-2
　　　1. Hussein, Saddam, 1937---Juvenile literature. 2. Presidents--Iraq--Biography--Juvenile literature. [1. Hussein, Saddam, 1937- 2. Presidents--Iraq.] I. Title. II. Series.

DS79.66.H87W48 2003
956.7044'092--dc21
[B]
　　　　　　　　　　　　　　　　　　　　2003050305

TABLE OF CONTENTS

A Fight to the End 5

Childhood Poverty 7

Dream of Arab Unity 9

Exile 12

Young Revolutionary 15

A New Agenda 18

War with Iran 21

Invading Kuwait 25

Rebuilding 28

Butcher of Baghdad 31

Loyalty or Death 33

Axis of Evil 36

Under Attack 40

Web Sites 43

Timeline 44

Fast Facts 46

Glossary 47

Index 48

On March 17, 2003, President Bush addressed the nation. He discussed the situation in Iraq and told President Saddam Hussein to accept exile or face military force.

A FIGHT TO THE END

ew people were surprised when the United States attacked Iraq in March 2003. President George W. Bush had been warning of an attack for months. In the days before the war, President Bush made it clear what he wanted. He wanted Iraqi president Saddam Hussein to leave Iraq.

No one was surprised at the targets of the first missiles, either. All of them were aimed at important buildings in Baghdad, Iraq's capital. The buildings were places where Saddam and his top aides could have been.

Hours later, Saddam appeared on Iraq's state-run television system. The stocky man with his dark mustache appeared pale in his military uniform. He called the bombings something criminals would do. He promised Iraq would win the battle against the United States and its allies. He asked the Iraqi people to defend their nation.

Saddam's speech did not surprise anyone. People who knew him said he would never back down. Saddam gained his power by being a man of action. He had long dreamed of being the greatest leader in the Arab world, and he was ready to do whatever it took to see his dream come true. Even his name means "he who confronts."

The *Wall Street Journal* once described Saddam as being like Jekyll and Hyde. On one hand, he can be a charming, persuasive man who is a devoted father to his five children. On the other hand, for the past 30 years, he has brutally killed anyone who got in his way.

Iraqi president Saddam Hussein appears on television March 20, 2003, three hours after the United States launched a war to overthrow him.

CHILDHOOD POVERTY

Saddam Hussein was born Saddam al-Tikriti on April 28, 1937. His home was a mud hut in the village of al-Auja, Iraq, near Tikrit. Saddam changed his last name to his father's first name when he was a young adult. He thought a different name would make it harder for his enemies to find him.

The details of Saddam's childhood have never been clear. Some people believe bandits killed Saddam's father, Hussein al-Majid, before the boy was born. Others say he deserted Saddam before the child's birth.

Saddam's mother, Subha al-Talfah, got help from her brother, Khairallah Talfah, when she found herself alone with a new baby. Talfah was a former Iraqi army officer. He taught young Saddam many things. He was one of the most important people in Saddam's life.

Subha remarried when Saddam was still young. Her second husband, Ibrahim al-Hassan, was a peasant farmer who tended sheep. Saddam said his stepfather was mean to him. Saddam said al-Hassan beat him and made him work all the time.

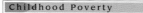

Often, Saddam sold melons on the street for his stepfather. Saddam also said he had to steal eggs and chickens both to sell and to eat.

Al-Hassan also did not let Saddam go to school, which made Saddam angry. His friends were learning to read while he was not. It is believed Saddam spent part of his childhood living this hard life with his mother and al-Hassan. He spent the other part with his uncle Talfah.

Saddam left al-Auja for good when he was nine or ten. He moved in with his uncle Talfah in Tikrit. There, children teased Saddam because he did not have a father. Saddam quickly learned how to defend himself. Sometimes he even hit his enemies with an iron bar he often carried.

In Tikrit, Saddam began to attend school. He finally learned to read. He was an average student at the Tikrit Secondary School for Boys. Yet, he is remembered as having big plans even then. A childhood friend of Saddam's recalled that most students in Tikrit wanted to be teachers. But not Saddam. He wanted to change Iraq.

DREAM OF ARAB UNITY

Iraq had been an independent country for just a few years when Saddam was born. Before then the United Kingdom controlled it. Many Iraqi people did not want the United Kingdom to have power. They wanted Iraqis to govern Iraq. They also hoped that all Arab nations could work together. And they wanted non-Arab countries to let Arabs rule themselves. People called this dream Arab nationalism.

Saddam's uncle Talfah believed strongly in Arab nationalism. He had lost his army job when he helped with a coup attempt against the British government. Talfah did not like the British. He disliked them even more after the coup attempt failed. Much of this anti-British feeling rubbed off on young Saddam.

Saddam also heard his uncle and others talk often about Arab nationalism. Saddam dreamed of a day when Arab nations would work together. He wanted them to be as powerful as the United Kingdom or the United States.

Around age 16, Saddam applied to the Baghdad Military Academy. But he failed the entrance exam and the school

A portrait of Saddam Hussein

rejected his application. So Saddam moved to Baghdad with his uncle and attended al-Karkh High School. Soon, he found himself more interested in politics than schoolwork.

It was not long before Saddam decided to follow in his uncle's footsteps. He took part in a coup attempt against Iraq's King Faisal II in 1956. King Faisal was friendly with Western nations. This upset Iraqis who supported Arab nationalism. The coup attempt was not successful, and the following year, Saddam joined the new Baath political party.

The Baath party had three main goals. Party members wanted all Arab nations to work together. They wanted non-Arab countries to leave the Arab world. And they wanted a socialist form of government.

EXILE

Saddam married a young woman named Sajida Talfah when he was in his early 20s. Sajida was Saddam's first cousin. The couple's families had arranged the marriage when Saddam was only four or five years old. Saddam and Sajida would have five children, three girls and two boys.

Saddam was still working to gain political power. By now, King Faisal II was no longer in power. He was assassinated in a coup in 1958. This meant Iraq had a new leader, General Abdul Kassem. Baath party members disliked Kassem. He had sought extra power by teaming up with communist supporters. Baath party members did not want Iraq to be communist. So in 1959, they began plotting to kill Kassem.

Baath party leaders needed a group of assassins to carry out their plot. One of them was young Saddam. Saddam was already known as a killer. He had spent six months in prison after being accused of murder. Saddam was building a violent reputation.

Saddam and a group of others tried to assassinate Kassem. They shot at Kassem as he rode down the street. A gunfight

broke out, and the group killed the driver of Kassem's car and one of his helpers. However, they failed to kill Kassem.

Saddam's role in the murder attempt has become an Iraqi legend. Saddam says he was shot in the leg. He says he dug the bullet out with a knife, disguised himself, swam across a river, and escaped from police as they chased him through the desert. Other sources say Saddam's wound came from another Baath fighter, that he caught a ride in the getaway car, and that a doctor helped him right away.

Whatever the truth about the event, after the attempt on Kassem's life, Saddam went into exile in Syria. Meanwhile, word spread about his role in the assassination attempt. Kassem's government threatened Saddam. Officials said he would be killed if he returned to Iraq. Egyptian president Gamal Abdel Nasser heard the story, too. Like Saddam, Nasser supported Arab nationalism. He invited Saddam to spend some time in Egypt.

General Abdul Kassem (right) sits with his deputy premier Abdul Salam Muhammad Arif.

YOUNG REVOLUTIONARY

Saddam stayed in Egypt for about three years as a guest of the government. Saddam used his time in exile to finish high school. He graduated at age 24, and entered Cairo University, where he studied law. However, he did not finish his studies there.

Saddam became more and more involved in politics. He joined Egypt's Baath party. He spent a lot of time in restaurants reading newspapers. Twice, police arrested him for threatening other students. Sources say he pulled a knife on a student who disagreed with him. People who knew him in Egypt recall he spent a lot of time alone, usually reading. They recall him as a loner and a troublemaker.

In 1963, a group of Baath party members and army officers overthrew Kassem's government and killed Kassem. Abdul Salam Muhammad Arif, an army officer, took control of Iraq's government. Saddam soon returned to Iraq. He helped Baath members question people suspected of supporting Kassem. Sometimes he tortured the people while he questioned them.

Often, Baath party members killed the people after torturing them. Saddam became skilled at torturing and killing people. Those talents helped him land an important job in the Baath party.

Arif soon took over the government completely with the help of the army. Saddam and his friends had to go into hiding again. There, they planned how they would take over Iraq. Saddam again participated in a coup attempt, but it failed. The police captured Saddam, and he spent two years in jail.

Eventually, Saddam escaped. He and several other prisoners got to leave the prison for an appointment. They talked their guard into stopping at a restaurant on the way back to the prison. At the restaurant, they excused themselves to go to the restroom. Then, they snuck out the back door and slipped away.

Saddam returned to his work with the Baath party. Soon, he was head of the party's internal security. The security system spied on people. They found people who disagreed with the Baath party and killed them. Saddam was very good at organizing this secret police force. It would become the basis for his power in later years.

Iraqi president Saddam Hussein fires shots into the air on December 31, 2000, during what may have been the biggest military parade in Baghdad since the 1991 Persian Gulf War.

A NEW AGENDA

The late 1960s saw more changes in the Middle East. In 1967, Israel captured lands from Egypt, Jordan, and Syria during the Six Day War. Iraq opposed Israel in the war and so did Saddam. He would always view Israel as an enemy of the Arab world.

In 1968, the Baath party gained control of Iraq's government. Saddam volunteered to be in charge of internal security. Internal security was a dirty job. No one else wanted to do it. It meant spying on people and killing them. Saddam did not mind. He quickly learned how to find and stop anyone who threatened the Baath government. He built an extensive network of people who spied on others and told Saddam what they learned.

Major General Ahmed Hassan al-Bakr was Iraq's new president. He was a distant relative of Saddam's. He and Saddam were from the same hometown. Saddam became second-in-command to al-Bakr in 1969. He held that position for 10 years. He often worked 18-hour days.

Those years were a mix of good and bad for the people of Iraq. Al-Bakr and Saddam worked to modernize the country.

Iraq had large supplies of crude oil. Al-Bakr and Saddam sold the oil and used the money to build roads, houses, and hospitals. They improved the country's water system and its farming system. They started a program to teach every Iraqi how to read. The United Nations (UN) even honored Iraq for its successful reading program.

At the same time, Saddam continued to use his spies. Many people wanted the Baath party out of the government. People opposed to the government tried to kill Saddam and al-Bakr in 1973. They failed, and Saddam got even. He captured people suspected of opposing him and had them killed.

Saddam enjoyed his power. People always gave him what he wanted. They feared they would be killed if they did not. For example, Saddam had never finished law school in Cairo. So he went to a Baghdad law school with four bodyguards carrying guns, and the school officials gave him the law degree. He also made up for being rejected by the military academy by making himself a military general.

Saddam also used his power to make himself rich. He controlled many businesses, including some that sold oil. Saddam used his spies and security forces to take over other businesses. The Hussein family had fine clothes, beautiful homes, and delicious food. Finally, Saddam had the money he never had as a peasant child in Tikrit.

Saddam Hussein speaks in the early 1980s. At the height of his regime, Saddam controlled the Iraqi media as well.

WAR WITH IRAN

In the late 1970s, al-Bakr was talking with leaders of Syria about a possible political union between Syria and Iraq. The two countries had already signed an agreement to begin joining their two militaries. As vice president, however, Saddam did not like these developments. He thought they threatened his dream of eventually becoming Iraq's leader. Saddam thought it was time for him to take over as the leader of Iraq.

Al-Bakr resigned suddenly in July 1979. He said his health was too bad to continue as president. In reality, Saddam had forced him out. Many people in the government were loyal to Saddam. They did what Saddam wanted, not what al-Bakr wanted. Saddam wanted to be president of Iraq. As before, he got what he wanted. He rounded up the people who had been loyal to al-Bakr, and he had them killed by firing squad.

The people of Iraq, however, saw a different image of their new president. They did not see him killing people. Instead, they saw him on television doing helpful things. He might be shown helping a farmer with the harvest or handing out candy to children. He had songs and poems written about him. Saddam also had his picture posted all around Iraq. He even appeared in the *Guinness Book of Records* for having more portraits of himself made than any other world leader.

Meanwhile, Iraq's economy was doing well. The country had many new buildings. People received free education and medical care. But Saddam still controlled what his people heard and what they said. He banned many non-Iraqi newspapers and broadcasts. He also made it a crime to own a typewriter without a special license.

Saddam made world headlines in September 1980, when he ordered the Iraqi military to invade Iraq's neighbor, Iran. Iran had recently undergone a revolution. Iran's new leader was named Ayatollah Khomeini. Saddam thought the Iranian leader was a threat to his power. So Saddam invaded Iran to stop Khomeini from doing anything that might take Saddam from power. One of Saddam's good friends and advisers urged him not to invade Iran. Saddam killed him for his opinion.

The Iran-Iraq War lasted eight years. The war took the lives of hundreds of thousands of people. Saddam was surprised at how well the Iranians fought. He had thought it would be an easy win for Iraq, yet the war dragged on. Saddam asked his advisers if he should withdraw. He wanted them to say no. His health minister said yes. Later, the health minister's family

Iraqi soldiers at Khorramshahr watch as smoke rises in the distance during the war with Iran in 1981. The port of Khorramshahr was the scene of heavy fighting during the Iran-Iraq War.

received a bag. Inside the bag was what was left of the minister's body. In the end, both countries agreed to a cease-fire.

Saddam was angry over the defeat, and he continued his aggression. This time, however, it was on his own people. For example, he killed many Kurds. The Kurds are a cultural tribe of people living in northern Iraq. The Kurds have long wanted their own nation. Many of the Kurds in Iraq had supported Iran in the war. They had hoped Iran would win so they could get their own country for good.

Saddam's military attacked the Kurds at the end of the war. Saddam ordered his soldiers to use chemical weapons on them. Thousands of Kurds died in the attacks. Thousands more had health problems because of the chemicals. Hundreds of thousands had to leave the country.

The vicious attacks drew international attention. People took a closer look at Saddam. Their thoughts of a smiling, helpful Saddam were replaced. They realized Saddam was a cold-blooded killer.

INVADING KUWAIT

Eight years of war with Iran had taken its toll on Iraq's economy. Iraq was now deeply in debt. Saddam needed money, so he turned to another neighbor. This one was oil-rich Kuwait. Kuwait had loaned Iraq money during the Iran-Iraq War. Saddam wanted Kuwait's officials to say he did not have to pay them back. Instead, the Kuwaiti officials asked for their money back.

Saddam said that Kuwait was really a part of Iraq. He said he wanted Kuwait back. He knew if he took over Kuwait, he could avoid repaying the loan. And he could get Kuwait's oil money.

Iraqi tanks invaded Kuwait on August 2, 1990. Iraq's 120,000 soldiers quickly defeated Kuwait's 20,000 fighters. The invasion was complete in a matter of days. Iraqis killed and hurt many Kuwaiti people and stole their belongings.

World leaders could not stay silent while watching events unfold in Kuwait. The UN scolded Saddam for his actions.

Twenty-eight nations, including the United States, decided to act. They assembled a force to drive Saddam's army out of Kuwait.

Operation Desert Storm, the aerial attack on Iraq's forces, began in January 1991. Coalition forces, led by the United States, had driven the Iraqis out of Kuwait by late February. Saddam lost thousands of soldiers in the fighting. He also lost much of his military equipment. Iraqi officials agreed to a cease-fire on February 27, 1991. Saddam did not attend. He refused to admit Iraq had lost the Persian Gulf War.

After the war, the UN issued economic sanctions against Iraq. The sanctions said no one could do business with Iraq. That left Iraq with no way to earn money. The people of Iraq faced starvation. Their country had vast fields of crude oil. But the people could not eat oil. They had to survive on only a little wheat, rice, flour, and tea.

Meanwhile, Saddam and his family had plenty to eat. His network of spies continued to kill anyone who dared speak against him. Saddam said it was not his fault that his people were starving. He blamed the UN and Western nations for the people's suffering.

U.S. and Iraqi military officials discuss cease-fire conditions at a peace conference on March 3, 1991, as Operation Desert Storm was nearing its end.

REBUILDING

Iraq is a nation of many different groups of people. There are Kurds in the north, Shiite Muslims in the south, and Sunni Muslims in central Iraq. Neither the Shiites nor the Kurds liked Saddam's leadership. They wanted a different leader who would keep their wants and needs in mind.

The Kurds and Shiites took advantage of the war in Kuwait. They hoped to rebel against Saddam's rule. U.S. president George H.W. Bush encouraged them. But Saddam still had soldiers and guns left after the war. Once again, he used them on his own people to crush the rebellion. Some believe Saddam killed between 30,000 and 60,000 Iraqis. In northern Iraq, more than one million Kurds fled the country. They knew they had to leave or be killed.

With the rebellion quashed, Saddam turned to rebuilding Iraq. He felt he needed to keep control now more than ever. He still wanted to be the major leader in the Arab world. Some Arabs still supported Saddam. They liked that he did things

Kurdish refugees in Turkey wash themselves while thousands of other refugees wait on the Iraqi side of the border for permission to cross.

without worrying what the United States would do. They wanted the Arab world to have power equal to that of Western nations. They saw Saddam working toward that.

Saddam had been very popular inside Iraq once, too. He had done good things for Iraq. But that was beginning to change. The people began to resent Saddam. The people of Iraq were the ones being killed. They were the ones starving.

An Iraqi store owner sells watches with pictures of Saddam on the faces.

BUTCHER OF BAGHDAD

Saddam's cruelty was well known inside Iraq. Over time, that information spread beyond Iraq's borders. Some people called Saddam the Butcher of Baghdad.

Saddam's actions and his image presented very different pictures. He plastered Iraq with smiling portraits of himself. Many of the people who worked for Saddam even had his picture on the face of their wristwatches. His birthday was made a national holiday in Iraq. Iraqi television showed movies about his life. It televised his speeches and people reading poetry that said good things about him. Photographs showed Saddam helping his kids with their homework.

In private, however, Saddam worried constantly about being killed. Some sources say he survived several attempts on his life. He used food tasters to test his food before he ate it. That way he could tell if the food was poisoned. He had 40 bodyguards to protect him. He had at least three men who looked just like him, called doubles. He sent these doubles in his place at public appearances where someone might have shot him. At home,

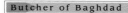

Saddam even feared germs. Reporters who met with Saddam said he made them wash their hands before meeting him.

Saddam also enjoyed an extravagant lifestyle. After the Persian Gulf War, Saddam built 48 plush palaces. He owned a yacht and liked to smoke expensive cigars. Some sources say he had four wives. He loved fancy clothes, including costumes and military uniforms.

Signs of Iraqi president Saddam Hussein can be found throughout Iraq.
This is just one of Saddam's presidential palaces in Baghdad.

LOYALTY OR DEATH

Over the years, many people have wanted Saddam dead. But he has made it nearly impossible for someone to get close enough to kill him. As a young man, Saddam studied the life of Joseph Stalin. Stalin was the Soviet Union's leader from 1929 to 1953. He was known for using threats and murder to maintain his power. Saddam modeled himself after Stalin.

People who have studied Saddam say his method is very effective. Saddam did not just kill the person he disliked, he killed that person's entire family—even their children. He regularly spied on everyone. He even spied on the few people he trusted. He believed that anyone could betray him at any time.

Saddam also used family ties to keep control of Iraq. Most of the top people in his government were friends and relatives. Saddam's oldest son, Uday, ran many committees. Saddam's second son, Qusay, ran his security system. Saddam's half-brother was also involved in the security system. Thousands of people from around Saddam's hometown held other important jobs.

Saddam Hussein speaks with elite members of his Republican Guard in Baghdad.

Many of them were criminals. All of those people had nothing without Saddam. They understood that they must keep Saddam in power to keep their own power.

Saddam used family ties to keep the military on his side, too. Saddam had to control the army or it could take away his power. Iraq's military had attempted many coups in the past. So Saddam made a special effort to put friends and family members in high army positions. He also created the Republican Guard, which was a group of elite soldiers. Their most important job was to protect Saddam and his government.

Saddam trusted few people. He did not hesitate to kill anyone he thought was a threat. It did not matter if they were a friend or family member. For example, two of his sons-in-law fled Iraq. They took their wives, Saddam's daughters, and their children with them. They sought safety in nearby Jordan. There, they told secrets of the bad things happening in Iraq. Saddam waited for a while. Then he told them to come back home. He said nothing would happen to them, so they returned to Iraq. The two sons-in-law were soon killed in a 13-hour gun battle.

AXIS OF EVIL

Saddam's violent actions did not go unnoticed. When Iraqi soldiers used chemical weapons against the Kurds and Iranians, they broke international rules for war. Those rules are called the Geneva convention. The UN demanded that Saddam get rid of his illegal weapons. They also demanded that inspectors be allowed to go to Iraq. The inspectors were to look for any weapons that were against the rules.

For years, Saddam tried to avoid weapons inspections. He refused to cooperate with the inspectors. Some people thought he hid weapons he did not want the inspectors to find, while also working on a nuclear bomb.

Experts believe Saddam began work on a nuclear weapon in the 1970s. Some say he got blueprints to build nuclear weapons from the United States. Saddam wanted the Arab world to have its own powerful weapons. He believed he was the right leader to do that. So he refused to back down, even to the UN.

The 1990s brought more fights between Iraq and the rest of the world. The United States launched several missiles at Iraq

This photograph shows what military officials describe as a truck filled with
Iraqi missiles found in Karbala, Iraq, by coalition forces on April 9, 2003.

Palestinian children march at a rally in support of Iraq
and Iraqi president Saddam Hussein.

in 1993. U.S. officials said Saddam had tried to have former U.S. president George H.W. Bush assassinated. The missile strikes were in retaliation for this.

More trouble came in 1994. Saddam ordered his troops to the Kuwaiti border. It looked like they were going to invade again. The United States and several other countries assembled soldiers there, too. For once, Saddam backed down.

The United States and the United Kingdom also fired missiles at Iraq in 1998 and 1999. Government officials said the missiles were meant to destroy military targets. Saddam fought back by not cooperating with weapons inspectors at all.

In 2002, Saddam faced a new enemy. U.S. president George W. Bush was the son of Saddam's old rival, George H.W. Bush. The young Bush had strong words against Saddam. He said Iraq was part of an axis of evil. Eventually, Bush took his message to the UN.

UNDER ATTACK

President George W. Bush addressed the UN in September 2002. He urged the UN to step up its enforcement of Iraqi sanctions. In November, it did. The UN Security Council approved Resolution 1441. It said that Saddam had to allow weapons inspectors to return to Iraq. If the Iraqi government did not cooperate, the resolution promised serious consequences.

UN weapons inspectors headed back to Iraq later that month. The U.S. government said that, once again, Saddam did his best to keep the inspectors from doing their jobs. His people cooperated only as much as they had to. His goal was to do just enough to avoid war. The U.S. government said Saddam did not really want weapons inspectors to see everything he had. President Bush threatened military action against Iraq, supported by Resolution 1441, if the Iraqi government continued not cooperating with the inspectors.

Some members of the UN said that the United States should not attack. They pointed out how the Iraqi people were already suffering. War would only make their suffering worse.

UN weapons inspectors wearing protective suits and gas masks prepare to enter a drug and medical appliance company on the outskirts of Baghdad on January 11, 2003.

The United Kingdom and the United States disagreed. They said Saddam's time was up. The Iraqi people needed their freedom. The United States and the United Kingdom began moving soldiers and weapons close to Iraq.

Saddam responded in his usual manner. In February 2003, he gave an interview and said Iraq would not back down. He said that the people of Iraq would defend their country and not give in to the United States. In March 2003, President Bush gave Saddam a choice. Saddam had to leave Iraq within 48 hours, or a coalition of nations would come together and, under Resolution 1441, use military force to disarm Iraq.

Those who knew Saddam well knew he would not leave. He would fight to the end, whatever that end might be. Forty-eight hours came and went. Saddam stayed in hiding, and missiles began soaring over Baghdad. Operation Iraqi Freedom had begun.

WEB SITES
WWW.ABDOPUB.COM

To learn more about Saddam Hussein, visit ABDO Publishing Company on the World Wide Web at **www.abdopub.com**. Web sites about Saddam Hussein are featured on our Book Links page. These links are routinely monitored and updated to provide the most current information available.

Operation Iraqi Freedom liberated the people of Iraq and toppled Saddam Hussein's regime.

TIMELINE

1937
Saddam Hussein born on April 28 in al-Auja, Iraq

1955
Moved to Baghdad with his uncle

1957
Joined the Baath party

1958
Married Sajida Talfah

1959
Attempted to kill Iraqi prime minister Kassem

1963
Returned to Iraq after exile in Cairo, Egypt

1969
Became second-in-command of Iraqi government

1979
Became leader of Iraq

1980
Began war with Iran

1988
Agreed to cease-fire in Iran-Iraq War

1990
Ordered invasion of Kuwait

1991
Forced to leave Kuwait

1998
Refused to cooperate with UN weapons inspectors

2003
Refused to leave Iraq under pressure of war by United States

FAST FACTS

Name: Saddam Hussein

Born: April 28, 1937

Birthplace: al-Auja, Iraq

Mother: Subha al-Talfah; she worked as a psychic.

Father: Hussein al-Majid; disappeared before Saddam Hussein was born.

Other Important Family Members: Khairallah Talfah, his uncle. Talfah was an officer in the army.

Education: Mustanseriya University in Baghdad and Cairo University; Saddam enrolled in both schools but didn't finish his education at either one.

Family Life: Married to Sajida, his cousin. She is the daughter of Khairallah Talfah. They have been married for 40 years. They have five children. Their daughters are Reghid, Rana, and Hala. Their two sons are Uday and Qusay.

Interests: Reportedly enjoys fishing.

Favorite Movies: *The Godfather*, *The Conversation*, and *The Day of the Jackal*.

Religion: Sunni Muslim. One Baghdad museum has a copy of the Muslim holy book, the Koran, written in Saddam's own blood. The book took three years to write.

Books written by Saddam Hussein: *Zabibah and the King* and *The Fortified Castle*.

Heroes: Winston Churchill and Joseph Stalin

WAR ★ IRAQ

GLOSSARY

Arab world:
Nations where a majority of the people are Arabs. Arabs share a common history, culture, and language. Arab nations are located in North Africa and the Middle East.

chemical weapons:
Poisonous agents, such as nerve gas, that may be released into the air to kill many people quickly.

communism:
A social and economic system in which everything is owned and operated by the government and is distributed to the people as needed.

coup:
The sudden, violent overthrow of a government by a small group of people.

exile:
To be expelled from one's home country.

firing squad:
A military unit assigned to carry out a sentence of death by shooting.

Muslim:
A person who follows Islam. Islam is a religion based on the teachings of the prophet Muhammad as they appear in the Koran. Shiite Muslims and Sunni Muslims make up two different branches of Islam.

prime minister:
The highest leader in parliamentary government.

revolution:
The overthrow of a government by its citizens. The old government is then replaced by a new one.

sanctions:
Measures taken against a nation that has disobeyed international law. Sanctions are meant to force the offending nation to obey the law.

socialism:
An economic system in which the government or the citizens control the production and distribution of goods.

INDEX

A

Arif, Abdul Salam Muhammad 15, 16

al-Auja, Iraq 7, 8

B

Baath party 11–13, 15, 16, 18, 19

Baghdad, Iraq 5, 11, 19, 31, 42

Baghdad Military Academy 9

al-Bakr, Ahmed Hassan 18, 19, 21

Bush, George H.W. 28, 39

Bush, George W. 5, 39, 40, 42

C

Cairo University 15

E

Egypt 13, 15, 18, 19

F

Faisal II (King) 11, 12

G

Geneva convention 36

H

al-Hassan, Ibrahim 7, 8

Hussein, Qusay 33

Hussein, Uday 33

I

Iran 22, 24, 25

Iran-Iraq War 22, 25

Israel 18

J

Jordan 18, 35

K

al-Karkh High School 11

Kassem, Abdul 12, 13, 15

Khomeini, Ayatollah 22

Kurds 24, 28, 36

Kuwait 25, 26, 28

M

al-Majid, Hussein 7

N

Nasser, Gamal Abdel 13

O

Operation Desert Storm 26

Operation Iraqi Freedom 42

P

Persian Gulf War 26, 32

R

Republican Guard 35

Resolution 1441 40, 42

S

Shiite Muslim 28

Soviet Union 33

Stalin, Joseph 33

Sunni Muslim 28

Syria 13, 18, 21

T

Talfah, Khairallah 7–9, 11

al-Talfah, Subha 7, 8

Talfah, Sajida 12

Tikrit, Iraq 7, 8, 19

Tikrit Secondary School for Boys 8

U

United Kingdom 9, 39, 42

United Nations (UN) 19, 25, 26, 36, 39, 40

United States 5, 9, 26, 28, 30, 36, 39, 40